curious about

MAKO SHARKS

BY DEBRA RANDORF

AMICUS LEARNING

What are you

curious about?

CHAPTER THREE

Life in the Ocean

Curious About is published by
Amicus Learning, an imprint of Amicus
P.O. Box 227, Mankato, MN 56002
www.amicuspublishing.us

Editor: Ana Brauer
Series Designer: Kathleen Petelinsek
Book Designer and Photo Researcher: Sara Hood

Library of Congress Cataloging-in-Publication Data
Names: Randorf, Debra, author.
Title: Curious about mako sharks / by Debra Randorf.
Description: Mankato, MN : Amicus Learning, an imprint of Amicus, [2026] | Series: Curious about sharks | Includes bibliographical references and index. | Audience: Ages 6–9 | Audience: Grades 2–3 | Summary: "How fast are mako sharks? Learn about this extraordinary ocean animal in this question-and-answer book for elementary-aged readers. Includes infographics, table of contents, glossary, books and websites for further research, and index"— Provided by publisher.
Identifiers: LCCN 2024048302 (print) | LCCN 2024048303 (ebook) | ISBN 9798892005067 (library binding) | ISBN 9798892005609 (paperback) ISBN 9798892006149 (ebook)
Subjects: LCSH Mako sharks—Juvenile literature.
Classification: LCC QL638.95.L3 R363 2026 (print) | LCC QL638.95.L3 (ebook) | DDC 597.3/3—dc23/eng/20241226
LC record available at https://lccn.loc.gov/2024048302
LC ebook record available at https://lccn.loc.gov/2024048303

Photo Credits: Alamy Stock Photo/KELVIN AITKEN / VWPICS, 15, Mark Conlin, 18–19, Masa Ushioda, 11; Blue Planet Archive/ Andy Murch, 12–13, Rodrigo Friscione, 8 (bottom); Getty Images/ Julian Gunther, 20–21, Mark Chivers, 14, Richard Robinson, 8 (top), Ronald C. Modra, 2, 7; Shutterstock/Jessica Heim, cover, 1, Martin Prochazkacz, 2, 5, Xavier ELIAS Photography, 3, 16–17; The Noun Project/Arthur Shlain, 22, 23, farra nugraha, 22, ridhobadal, 23; Vecteezy/om1947, 10

CHAPTER ONE

Why are they called mako sharks?

Because of their teeth! Mako means "shark tooth" in the **Māori** language. Mako sharks have many sharp teeth. You can even see their teeth when their mouth is closed! A mako shark is blue on the top and white on the bottom. It swims faster than any other shark.

DID YOU KNOW?

Sharks grow new teeth throughout their life. If they lose one, a new one will grow.

A mako shark is a great hunter.

How fast is a mako shark?

Very fast! The mako shark is the fastest shark in the world. It can swim up to 45 miles (72 kilometers) per hour. They have special **scales** that help them swim fast. The scales are close together and help the sharks move through the water.

MAKO SHARKS: ATHLETES OF THE OCEAN!

Distance swimmer:
2,000 miles (3,129 km) in a year

Fastest shark:
up to 45 mph (72 km/h)

High jumper:
up to 20 ft (6 meters)

A mako shark will jump out of the water when it hunts.

Shortfin mako sharks are faster than longfin makos.

Longfin mako sharks are rare and hard to find.

How big is a mako shark?

They can grow up to 14 feet (4.3 m) long. There are two types of mako sharks, the shortfin mako and the longfin mako. The longfin mako has longer fins and a slimmer body. The shortfin mako is more common.

CHAPTER TWO

Can I swim with one?

It's not recommended! Mako sharks live in warm, deep water. They do not swim close to shore. But beware. It is a **fierce** shark that you do not want to meet. They might think you are there for lunch!

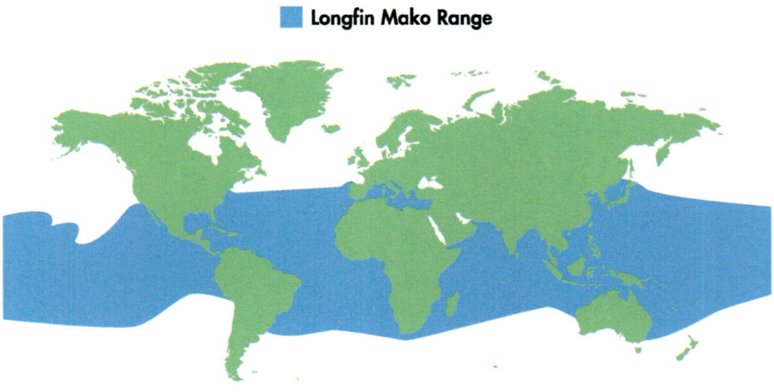

Makos often swim long distances across oceans.

Mako sharks have many razor-sharp teeth.

How do mako sharks hunt?

Mako sharks are great hunters. They swim many miles (kilometers) to find food. They have good eyesight. They can sense the movements of other fish. A mako shark can jump up to 20 feet (6 m) out of the water when chasing **prey**.

What do mako sharks eat?

Makos are at the top of the ocean **food chain**.

A mako shark will eat anything that swims. They eat squid, schools of fish, and even other sharks. Sometimes they eat sea turtles. They use their long, sharp teeth to grab and eat their prey.

WHAT'S ON THE MENU?

Mako shark teeth are like hooks. They trap prey so it can't get away.

How are mako shark babies born?

Mako shark babies grow in their mother's body for a year and a half before birth. They are born in groups of four to six. The babies are about 2 feet (0.6 m) long when born. This large size helps them **survive**.

A baby mako shark is called a pup.

Do mako sharks swim together?

A mako might swim with another shark if there is lots of food around.

Not really. Makos like to swim and hunt alone. They swim long distances to find fish to eat. Makos can swim up to 90 miles (145 km) a day. They usually only swim together in the spring or fall to **mate**.

Makos can live up to 30 years in the wild.

Are mako sharks endangered?

DID YOU KNOW?
As of 2022, it is against the law for US fishers to catch a mako shark in the Atlantic Ocean.

Yes. Makos are threatened by overfishing. Many people enjoy their meat. Their fins are made into soup. Mako sharks are also caught by accident in the large nets of fishing boats. This causes their numbers to drop.

STAY CURIOUS!

ASK MORE QUESTIONS

What is special about mako shark teeth?

What other sharks swim fast?

Try a BIG QUESTION: How can humans protect mako sharks?

SEARCH FOR ANSWERS

Search the library catalog or the Internet.
A librarian, teacher, or parent can help you.

Using Keywords
Find the looking glass.

Keywords are the most important words in your question.

If you want to know about:

- where to find makos, type: MAKO SHARK OCEANS
- what sharks swim the fastest, type: FAST SHARKS

LEARN MORE

FIND GOOD SOURCES

Here are some good, safe sources you can use in your research.
Your librarian can help you find more.

Books

Mako Sharks
by Julie Murray, 2024.

Shark: Apex Predator
by Ruth A. Musgrave, 2023.

Internet Sites

Britannica Kids | Mako Shark
https://kids.britannica.com/kids/article/mako-shark/639028
Britannica Kids has fact-checked articles about many different animals.

Kiddle | Shortfin Mako Shark Facts for Kids
https://kids.kiddle.co/Shortfin_mako_shark
Kiddle is an online encyclopedia for kids with facts on many topics.

Every effort has been made to ensure that these websites are appropriate for children. However, because of the nature of the Internet, it is impossible to guarantee that these sites will remain active indefinitely or that their contents will not be altered.

SHARE AND TAKE ACTION

Host a shark week at your school.
Share posters about mako sharks and other cool sharks you have studied.

Plastic and other trash are bad for our water.
Plan a beach clean-up with your friends and family.

Create a shark trivia game.
Write down all the facts you have learned about mako sharks and quiz your friends or classmates.

GLOSSARY

fierce Extremely wild or violent.

food chain A series of plants and animals in which each uses the next in the series as a food source.

Māori The indigenous people of New Zealand.

mate To pair up to produce young.

prey An animal hunted by another animal for food.

scale A small, stiff, flat plate found on the skin of a fish.

survive To continue to live despite threats to one's life.

INDEX

About the Author

Debra Randorf lives and works in Minneapolis, Minnesota. She is so curious, she goes to the library at least once a week.